Dedications

This book is dedicated to my wife and children, and the loving memory of my parents.

Acknowledgements

I would like to gratefully acknowledge as many of the individuals in my life who contributed to the original idea, creation, revision, and final publication of this book. Foremost, a heartfelt thanks to my devoted wife, Sheryl, for her love, patience and tolerance. She helped in so many ways, and co-published this book with me. To my children, who heard me say innumerable times "I'm going to pull off to the side of the road for just one more picture." To my kindred spirit, my brother by choice – John Hays, who kept both of my oars in the water even when I hit dry land, who always believed in me, and who planted the seed for this book. To the many unique, interesting, and special characters of Tybee Island who own the buildings, properties and landmarks and who gave me the privilege of photographing The Hidden Treasures of our island. A special thanks to Amin Mohandeshi the graphic designer of the book. Lastly, I am deeply grateful to my *paesano* and dear friend "Spaghetti Rich" Sestili, the creative director, organizer, and savior of the entire project when I had given up all hope. Also, to Davidson & Company for their generous professional support of this entire endeavor. Finally, I want to thank you for purchasing this book and contributing to these very worthwhile organizations.

All profit from this book will go directly to benefit the children of these non-profit organizations: Chatham Academy at Royce, Savannah, Georgia, and The Marine Science Center of Tybee Island.

Gustave "Stavie" Kreh, M.D.

The Thrill of Tybee Island

Located just 18 miles east of Savannah, Georgia, on US 80, is the beginning of The Thrill of Tybee. As you enter the island along the expressway, roll down those windows and enjoy the beauty of the wild green marshes, the sweet-salty air, and the rows of gorgeous purple and white oleanders on each side of the highway. Slow down to enjoy the absolute beauty, knowing this is where the journey into our wonderful dream begins.

Introduction

The book **Tybee Island: The Hidden Treasure** is a lavish photographic tribute to the power, mystique, and grace of the area. This elegant coffee-table book features Dr. Gustave Kreh's intriguing and unique nature photography, collected over several years on a quest to capture the spirit of the low country.

Tybee Island is a place where the salt waters co-mingle with the land to create a treasure that is pristine and rich in natural beauty – soft winds whisper through Spanish moss, Loggerhead turtles nest, egrets wade and pelicans soar.

"I have come to truly appreciate the natural beauty of Georgia's northernmost barrier island. The sea marsh separating the mainland from Tybee Island is awash with glorious sunrises and sunsets, commercial shrimp boats, recreational kayakers, migratory and resident birds and even a military historic fort. It is my desire to share the beauty, history and meaning of this wonderful island with diverse photographs and some historical text, but mostly I'll let the pictures speak for themselves".

Intro article written by John A. Hays, Jr., Ph.D. longtime friend of "Stavie"

Florence Martus

The Famous Waving Girl of Savannah-Tybee Island

The legends abound concerning Florence Martus and why she waved her large pillow case, (some say a handkerchief) greeting ships as they entered the South Channel of the Savannah River. Yet one legend has outlived all the rest. It tells of a sailor from Boston, who met Florence in 1888, on Cockspur Island, and after three days the two of them fell in love. He asked for her hand in marriage and she promised to be faithful to him, waiting for his return. Florence waved her pillowcase by day and lantern by night, to each passing ship, hoping that one of them would be the vessel carrying her lover. She kept waving for fifty years, looking for him to return, but he never did.

A large statue of her, with one of her many faithful collies, stands on River Street in Savannah today.

FLORENCE MARTUS
1869 — 1943
SAVANNAH'S WAVING GIRL

History

A short history of the island.

Most historians believe "Tybee" derives from the Native American Euchee Indian word for "salt" which was one of many natural resources found on Tybee.

In the early days of the Island, many different countries explored Tybee Island, giving rise to our theme of TYBEE ISLAND: THE HIDDEN TREASURE.

In 1520 Lucas Vasquez de Ayllon laid claim to Tybee as part of Spain's "La Florida" which extended from the Bahamas to Nova Scotia.

Then came the French in 1605, also looking for riches, but this time it was sassafras root, that Europeans called the miracle cure. Later, the Spanish fought the French in a naval battle just off shore and prevailed.

For many decades pirates visited the Island in search of a safe haven and hiding place for treasure. Tybee and remote islands like it would also be a source for fresh water and game to replenish supplies.

Spain would be forced to eventually give up their claim to Tybee due to superior French and British settlements. In 1733 General James Oglethorpe and a handful of settlers came to the area. Here they established the new colony which would be named to honor King George. General Oglethorpe ordered a lighthouse constructed to mark the entrance to the river in 1736, and a small fort to be constructed to insure control over access to the river.

In 1736 John Wesley, the "Father of Methodism," said his first prayer on the American Continent at Cockspur Island.

Tybee would play a significant role throughout Georgia and U.S. history, including the Revolutionary War, when Tybee served as the staging area for French Admiral D'Estaing's ill fated 1779 Siege of Savannah, when combined multinational forces attempted to defeat the British held Savannah.

During the War of 1812, the Tybee Island Lighthouse was used as a signal tower to warn Savannah of possible attack by the British.

By the outbreak of the American Civil War, Tybee would again play an important military role in U.S. history. First Confederates occupied the Island. In December of 1861, the Rebel forces would withdraw to Fort Pulaski under orders from Robert E. Lee to defend Savannah and the Savannah River. Union forces under the Command of Quincy Adams Gilmore took control of Tybee and began constructing cannon batteries on the west side of Tybee facing Fort Pulaski about one mile away. On April 11th, 1862, those cannon batteries would fire a new weapon called "Rifled Cannon" at Fort Pulaski and change forever the way the world protected its coastal areas. Within 30 hours, the rifled guns had such a devastating effect on the brick fort that it was surrendered and all forts like Pulaski were considered obsolete. Devastation to the walls of the fort are still visible today

Thirty two years after the end of the Civil War, work on Fort Screven began. Its purpose was to provide a more modern system of seacoast defenses. Six, poured concrete, low profile, gun batteries and a minefield were ordered for Tybee along with hundreds of other military buildings. Gun Batteries, such as Battery Garland would be named to honor America's war heroes. From 1897 to 1947, Fort Screven would be an integral part of America's Coastal Defense system. Troops would train and stand guard on Tybee through the Spanish American War of 1898, World War I, and World War II. In 1947, the Fort was closed and sold to the Town of Tybee and tourism became a major part of Tybee's history.

Tybee Ft. Pulaski

Cockspur Island

The Heroics of Cockpsur Island Lighthouse

Cornelius Mather, who served as the Keeper 1851-1853, capsized his boat and drowned in the cold February waters leaving his widow Mary to take care of the little light. Tragedy struck again in 1854 when the structure was destroyed by a hurricane. The tower was rebuilt and enlarged on the same foundation the next year.

August, 1871, Keeper Patrick Eagan and his sons Michael and Thomas tried to service the beacon during a severe storm. Their boat capsized. Mr. Eagan and his son Michael held tight to the boat and beached on a nearby barrier island. Thomas drowned; his body was never recovered.

Fort Pulaski
National
Monument
Cockspur Island

South Channel

Lighthouse

North Beach

Fort Screven

Blackbeard's
Treasure

80

Savannah

516

South Carolina

80

Georgia

Tybee Island

TYBEE ISLAND

Tybee Pier
Savannah Beach

*Atlantic
Ocean*

Tybee Inns

There are several inns on Tybee Island, and all of them have great charm and atmosphere, filled with stories of romance and intrigue. Many stories involve well known officers who lived in these inns, and courted the eligible ladies of Savannah.

Pictured here are: Lighthouse Inn, Tybee Island Inn and Savannah Beach Inn

Tybee Lighthouse

Under the direction of Noble Jones of Wormsloe Plantation, work began on the first lighthouse built on Tybee Island. Completed in 1736 and made of wood, the first lighthouse stood ninety feet tall and was reported to be the tallest building of its kind in America.

The second Tybee lighthouse, like the first one, was constructed too close to the Atlantic Ocean and was threatened with destruction. In 1768, a third lighthouse was built, further away from the ocean.

In 1866, a new brick and cast iron lighthouse for Tybee was authorized. The lower sixty feet of the 1773 Tybee Lighthouse were used as the foundation of the fourth Tybee Lighthhouse. Ninety-four feet were added. The Lighthouse was one hundred and fifty-four feet tall, was re-classified as a major aid to navigation, and required three keepers to operate the light station.

In 1933, the fuel for the lighthouse was converted from kerosene to electricity. In 1939, the United States Coast Guard took over the operation of America's Lighthouses and occupied Tybee Light Station until 1987. Today the Light Station is operated by the Tybee Island Historical Society, which has begun a restoration campaign to return the entire light station to its historic early 20th century character.

Tybee Lighthouse Stamp

CAPE LOOKOUT, NORTH CAROLINA   MORRIS ISLAND, SOUTH CAROLINA   TYBEE ISLAND, GEORGIA   HILLSBORO INLET, FLORIDA   OLD CAPE HENRY, VIRGINIA

Tybee Island Light Station was selected for a commemorative stamp. It was issued on Friday, June 13th, 2003. The stamp was part of the third series of lighthouse stamps issued by the United States Postal Service.

The series featured five Southeastern Lighthouses: Old Cape Henry, Cape Lookout, Morris Island, Hillsboro Inlet, and Tybee lighthouses.

TYBEE ISLAND, GEORGIA

Ft. Screven

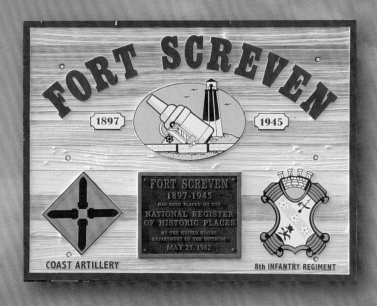

Battery Garland, (Tybee Island Museum) located across from Tybee Lighthouse, was built in 1899 and armed with 12-inch rifled guns. Battery Brumby, located next to Battery Garland, was built in 1898 and armed with four 8-inch guns on disappearing carriages, and was the only fortification finished in time for the Spanish-American War. These guns could fire 200-pound projectiles over 8 miles.

Battery Habersham, at Pulaski Street and Van Horn Drive, was armed in 1900 with eight 12-inch steel rifled mortars, the most devastating artillery at Fort Screven. These guns would fire 700-pound shells in a high arc from four or eight guns at a time, with the intention of landing shells on the deck of an enemy ship at once.

The concrete walls of some of these batteries are almost 20 feet thick, and engineers used the abundance of seashells on the island as a filler substitute for gravel in the concrete mixture.

Historians tell us that the infamous and brutal Blackbeard the Pirate, aka Edward Teach, stole what would be today millions in riches from wealthy passengers on merchant ships during the period of 1716 to 1718.

In a desperate survival move to escape the onslaught of the angered British Navy, Blackbeard escaped to the little known area of Tybee Island. Local folklore states, and some historians concur, that before he died he told one of his closest mates that he buried a sizeable chunk of gold coins, cups, plates, and emerald laden gold jewelry somewhere in the soft sands on the "northern-most tip of the island." That would put it very close to where this battery was built. The treasure has not been found to this date.

Happy digging maties.

Tybee *Beach*

TIME TO EAT

Tybee Pier

TYBRISA, CENTRAL OF GEORGIA RAILWAY'S DANCING AND BATHING PAVILION, TYBEE ISLAND, GA.

circa 1918 Copyright credit unknown

Built in 1891, by the Central of Georgia Railroad, and called The Tybrisa Pavilion, the pier stood for seventy-five years before burning down. The railroad used the original pier as a busy and fun-filled destination for vacationers. The beach and sun entertained the travelers during the day, and there was always great musical entertainment by well known "Big Bands" at night. The current pier was built and completed in time for the 1996 Olympics.

Tybee Marine Science

The Tybee Island Marine Science Center features marine life indigenous to the Georgia coast. The aquariums, exhibits, and actual experience in the ocean with nets, allow for an exciting day or week of marine life education. Discover a variety of fish, reptiles, invertebrates, corals, and other interesting sea creatures. Learn about barrier islands, the living Georgia state seashell, and horseshoe crabs. Compare turtles from the salt marsh and the sea. Try the popular "touch tank" that the children love so much.

Tybee Shrimp Boats

What an artist's dream to be able to paint the wonderful scenes created by the old wooden and majestic shrimp boats trudging through the Tybee waters.

Tybee Speed Boats

Vacationers as well as local residents pack the beach area in the summer to see these incredibly fast, and ultra loud, speedboats. Bring a cooler of food and drinks, a comfortable beach chair, and hold your breath.

Tybee Restaurants

There are numerous restaurants on the island. Whether you eat a hearty breakfast at The Breakfast Club, or lunch at Bahama Bob's, or Fannie's On The Beach, you will have a great meal and a memorable occasion. Try dinner with lively music at the North Beach Grill, or the unusual atmosphere and low country boil at The Crab Shack. For those looking for a more romantic theme, try George's, The Hunter House, or Tango's. Now this is something to write home about.

Tybee Night Life

Not much needs to be said. Just enjoy the music, fun, and the romantic moonlight. "Amore."

Tybee Flowers

"Espectacular," is how the early Spanish soldiers referred to the foliage on the island. Although they had seen colorful flowers in their own land, the salty marshes and hot dried sand dunes nurtured these unexpected, wild, colorful displays.

Tybee Beach Bum Parade

This parade is the zaniest, craziest, you will ever experience. Get ready to get wet. Every year the local "Beach Bums" serve up a pleasant surprise with the world's biggest waterfight. Here's a hint: Leave the BMW convertible at home, and don't squirt the police.

GRAND MARSHAL MAYOR WALTER PARKER

Don't miss it. Great food, great music, and always wonderful surprises from all of the local restaurants, on new and delicious seafood creations. The Festival strives to find the best bands for the two day event held in late August every year.

Tybee Birds

The Black Skimmers

The Black Skimmer (a species of special concern) generally breeds from May through September nesting in large colonies. It nests on barren beaches of sand, gravel or shells, on dry mudflats and salt-encrusted soils, and at gravel pits along rivers. Do Not Disturb them, please.

The Black Skimmer feeds on small fish and shrimp taken by skimming along the surface of the water and snatching their prey with a quick downward snap of their bill.

The Terns and Seagulls

Bird watching on Tybee is a wonderful pastime for the whole family. Many different, and often rare species, inhabit the beaches of Tybee and Little Tybee Island to the south. Beachgoers will have an enjoyable time with these comical and lively birds.

The Great Egret

What beauty and grace are displayed by the Great Egret, who abounds on the marshes of the Island.

Tybee St. Patty's

What a wonderful treat. Doctors, lawyers, indian chiefs, local politicians, and surprise celebrities all turn out for this festival. Everybody is Irish, as singing, dancing and outlandish costumes are the order of the day.

Tybee Houses

The houses on the island range from the simple and functional, to the magnificent. Pictured above is one of the very few remaining of the Officers Row houses, circa 1898. These houses, which were quarters for the unmarried officers of Ft. Screven, serve today as private residences and historic inns. They are much sought after for their incredible history and solid architecture of the period.

Tybee Cottages

As you drive around Tybee you will meet many unusual, talented and colorful characters, as well as the houses and shops they live and work in. Splashy orange, yellow, blue and purple are the norm for the cottages and shops. The tradition of painting with such lively colors goes back to early settlers who used color schemes for family identification.

FOR SALE
BY OWNER
Cottage For Sale
from the
Jane Coslick
Cottage Collection
844-5857

Another Historic
Cottage Restoration
Project by
JANE COSLICK

Tybee Butterflies

Like tiny, nervous, glittering jewels among the colorful flowers, the many different species of butterflies bring a soft, colorful life to Tybee.

Tybee Celebrities

The celebrities started coming to Savannah-Tybee with the making of the movies, FORREST GUMP and MIDNIGHT IN THE GARDEN OF GOOD AND EVIL. Once here they fell in love with the charm, history, and easy living of Savannah. It wasn't long before they found the beauty and magic of Tybee Island. Today, it is quite common to see well known actors, producers, directors and writers just strolling along the curvy beaches or having a meal at North Beach Grill.

There is an unwritten rule here for marine life and celebs: a polite "hello" or "how are you" and keep going. They are here for the same reason you are, to have fun with their families in a hassle free environment. The celebs have even been known to join in on pick-up volley ball games on the beach. No autographs, please. Tybee people are way above that.
"Hey, mom, guess who was on my team today?" Now is that cool or what?

Tybee Turtles

The Loggerheads

The marine life on Tybee is quite special. Several years ago, the famous and endangered Loggerhead turtles, found this beach and began developing nests. The female crawls onto the beach at night, lays her eggs, which can take all night, buries them and then heads back to the sea. A prodigious female can drop over 100 eggs in one night.

About sixty days later, baby Loggerheads two inches long push their snouts out of the cool night sand and follow the path to the sea as well. Over the years, if they survive, they can grow to 250 pounds, and three feet long. Red lights, which do not disorient the turtles, are used by scientists to observe the progress of the newborn.

There are signs all over the beach about Lights Out at Dusk. The car, street, or restaurant lights confuse the babies and seriously reduce the survival rate. Recently, Leatherback Turtles have also been visiting Tybee Island, which has added to the residents' excitement.

Do Not Disturb is the rule. What a fantastic site to see them follow the light of the summer moon bouncing off the gentle waves of the Atlantic Ocean.

TURTLE XING

Sea Turtles Aren't Afraid of the Dark.
Lights Out... 9 PM.
Tybee Island Marine Science Center 786 · 5917 (912)

photo credit: Dr. Bruce Carlson, Georgia Aquarium

Tybee Fireworks

The 4th of July is always a great treat with spectacular fireworks on the beach.

This is definitely one of the highlights of the summer. Just terrific.

Tybee Activities

Running, biking, swimming, fishing, rowing, kayaking, beach walking, kiting: There is no end to the fun and sun.

"We wanderers, ever seeking the lonelier way, begin no day where we have ended another day; and no sunrise finds us where sunset left us."

"Leave only your footprints"

The Hidden Treasure

By now you have realized that the true riches of The Hidden
Treasure are the golden sunsets, the silvery tips of the afternoon
waves of the Atlantic, the lush green emerald marshes, the natural
floral bouquets, the sweet-spicy salt air, and the wealth of history.
In order to truly enjoy this pictorial treasure you must now share
it with all of your loved ones and friends.

The Photographer and the Dream.
Dr. Gustave Kreh pictured here in 1978, as the young pediatrician who just discovered the magic of Tybee Island.

Dr. Kreh, graduated from the LSU School of Medicine in New Orleans in 1973, and completed a pediatric residency at the Baylor Affiliated Hospitals in Houston Texas in 1976. His dedication to duty followed graduation, serving as a Captain in the U.S. Army Medical Corps at Ft. Stewart, Georgia, from 1976-1978, receiving the Army Commendation Medal for his outstanding service. Stavie became a permanent fixture and an ambassador of Savannah, Georgia, by 1978. He married a Savannah native, the adorable Sheryl Karp. Together they raised two children. Stavie's entire professional life has been dedicated to the health needs, and well being of the children of Savannah. He has been a compassionate and talented pediatrician, a mentor to younger doctors, and a civic minded individual. Throughout the years, Stavie has been actively involved in several charitable organizations for a variety of well-known causes.

Amin Mohandesi   Rich Sestili

Creative Director / Editor.
Rich Sestili from Marietta, Ga., who studied Graphic Design at Carnegie Mellon University and later graduated from the University of Pittsburgh, accepted the challenge of editing through the thousands of photos from Dr. Kreh, creating a theme, and highlighting the magic of the Island.

Designer and the look.
Amin Mohandesi, a graduate of Atlanta College of Art, worked with Rich to develop a style that would be clean, simple, and memorable.

Color preparation of files and pre press:
Davidson & Co. Marietta, Ga.

Printed in Canada by Four Colour Imports, Ltd.

www.tybeetreasure.com

"Shalom"